Pocket Portfolio of Jokes, Definitions and Toasts for Numerous Popular Occasions

Reprinted from

SPEAKER'S ENCYCLOPEDIA OF HUMOR
Copyright 1961

NEW TREASURY OF STORIES FOR EVERY SPEAKING AND WRITING OCCASION
Copyright 1959

BRAUDE'S HANDBOOK OF HUMOR FOR ALL OCCASIONS
Copyright 1958

Prentice-Hall, Inc.
Englewood Cliffs, New Jersey

Collected and Edited by

JACOB M. BRAUDE

Printed in the United States of America

ISBN 0-13-683871-5

Pocket Portfolio of Jokes, Definitions and Toasts for Numerous Popular Occasions

Before you make your next speech, or just to liven up your conversation, pick up a few nuggets of wit from this handy little collection of jokes, definitions and toasts for numerous popular occasions.

As a speaker you know there's nothing like a burst of mirth to liven up your audience and win their attention and enthusiasm.

Here you'll find some of the most hilarious anecdotes, jokes, and stories that ever broke up an audience. In addition, you'll see a number of definitions to give your talk or point a humorous, ironic twist. And last, you'll get a number of witty toasts.

The three parts of the portfolio are each categorized to provide you with a large number of humor gems for many different occasions. Without any trouble at all, you will be able to work many of the jokes in this portfolio into almost any speech or speaking occasion.

Basically, there are three points in your talk where humor is not only welcome, but desirable, according to the country's best speakers.

The first point is at the very beginning of your talk. At this point your audience hasn't made up its mind, either about you or your talk. A little humor right at the beginning puts everyone at ease, gains you the audience's sympathy, attention, and enthusiasm.

The next point is within your talk. Here you can use humor to strengthen the theme of your speech, the main idea you are delivering. Often, you'll find that a humorous story, which people like to remember, will help carry your message far beyond the audience you are addressing.

The last point is, of course, the end of your speech. The audience's last impression of you is often the longest remembered. If you've stepped on any toes during your talk, here's the place to make everyone happy again.

Section 1

STORIES

Alcohol

I've drunk wine for seventy-five years, and I never drink water. I have a constitution of iron, and water rusts iron.

—André L. Simon

Returning from a trip to Europe, Mark Twain became annoyed as a customs official rummaged through his baggage. "My good friend," the author exclaimed, "you don't have to mix up all my things. There are only clothes in there—nothing but clothes."

But the suspicious fellow kept rooting around until he hit upon something hard. He pulled out a quart of the finest-quality bourbon. "You call this 'just clothes'?" cried the official.

"Sure thing," Twain replied calmly. "That is my nightcap."

Lincoln once replied to a prohibitionist's complaint that General Grant was overly fond of his bottle.

"Find out the brand of whiskey the General uses," Lincoln said. "I would like to furnish the same brand to my other generals."

Alcohol is something which often puts the wreck in recreation.

When a fellow comes down to the office Monday morning looking very haggard it's usually due to his weekend condition.

—Maurice Seitter

A physician, observing Charles Bannister, the great English actor, about to drink a glass of brandy, said: "Don't drink that filthy stuff; brandy is the worst enemy you have."

"I know that," responded Charles, "but you know we are commanded by scripture to love our enemies."

Church attendance

Churches should all be air conditioned; it is unhealthy for people to sleep in a stuffy room.

Some people must think the Sunday service is like a convention; many families just send one delegate.

The Vicar asked little Nellie the difference between an audience and a congregation. "An audience listens; a congregation doesn't."

The retiring usher was instructing his youthful successor in the details of his office. "And remember, my boy, that we have nothing but good, kind Christians in this church—until you try to put someone else in their pew."

"Just go out there and give your sermon with fire and determination. You're not afraid of the congregation, are you?"

"Oh, no," smiled the vicar. "The choir and I have them outnumbered."

Dad criticized the sermon, Mother thought the organist made a lot of mistakes. Sister didn't like the choir's singing. But they all shut up when Billy chipped in with the remark: "I think it was a darn good show for a dime."

Two ladies, dressed to the hilt in their Easter finery, were making slow progress in the crowd headed for the entrance to the church. Finally one of them burst out impatiently, "Now wouldn't you think that these people who do nothing but go to church Sunday after Sunday would stay home on Easter and leave room for the rest of us!"

A Saturday night backslider suddenly began attending church faithfully on Sunday mornings. The pastor was highly gratified and told him, "How wonderful it makes me feel to see you at services with your good wife!"

"Well, Parson," said the prodigal, "it's a matter of choice—I'd rather hear your sermon than hers."

American evangelist Billy Graham tells the amusing story of a fire which broke out in a small-town church.

When the fire brigade, siren wailing, arrived on the spot the minister recognized one of the men. "Hello, there, Jim—I haven't seen you in church for a long time," he chided.

"Well," answered the sweating man, struggling with the hose, "there hasn't been a fire in church for a long time."

Golf

Golf pro: "Now just go through the motions without hitting the ball."

Beginner: "That's precisely the trouble I'm trying to overcome."

First golfer: "Shall we play again next Saturday?"

Second golfer: "Well, I was going to get married on Saturday, but I can put it off."

One Saturday afternoon, the locker room boy answering the telephone heard a female voice say, "Is my husband there?"

The boy promptly answered, "No, ma'am."

"How can you say he isn't there before I even tell you who I am?"

"Don't make no difference, lady. They ain't never nobody's husband here."

Mistake

A worker was shorted two dollars in his pay envelope, and complained to the paymaster.

"You were overpaid two dollars last week and didn't object," reasoned the paymaster.

"I know," said the employee. "I don't mind overlooking one mistake, but when it happens the second time, I think it's time to complain."

A father had given his son a dollar for his birthday. All afternoon, the lad had trotted around his neighborhood, getting his bill changed to silver at the grocer's, back to a bill again at the baker's, and so on. Observing all this hustle and bustle, the father asked him the reason for his strange behavior.

"Well, you see, it's like this," replied the enterprising chap, "sooner or later somebody is going to make a mistake, and it's not going to be me."

"Look, madam," said the irate fellow who was strap-hanging on the bus, "you are standing on my foot."

"Oh, I am sorry," the lady standing next to him said. "I really thought it belonged to this man sitting down."

Psychiatry

A farmer brought his brother to see the psychiatrist. "My brother," he explained, "thinks he's a hen."

"Really," said the psychiatrist, "and how long has he been thinking on those lines?"

"For about four months," replied the farmer.

"And you did nothing about it?"

"No, doctor."

"That's too bad. Why in the name of all that's reasonable didn't you bring him to see me sooner?"

"Well, to tell you the truth, doctor, we needed the eggs."

The attractive woman psychiatrist was attending a convention. At one of the lectures the man sitting next to her began to pinch her. Annoyed, she was about to give him an angry retort, when she changed her mind.

"Why should I get angry?" she decided. "After all—it's his problem."

Romance

"You mean to say that you're engaged to five different boys at once?"

"Yeah, I can hardly wait until after Christmas to straighten things out."

"So you were engaged to Agnes for five years and then she gave you back your ring? That's what I call a cruel blow."

"Oh, it wasn't too bad. In fact, it worked out rather nicely. In the years that Agnes and I were engaged, the ring doubled in value and when she gave it back I was able to get a better girl with it."

Gloria: "I hear you have accepted him. Did he happen to mention that he had proposed to me first?"

Gwendolyn: "Not specifically. He did say, however, that he had done a lot of foolish things before he met me."

Hank: "You used to say there was something about me you couldn't help loving."

Claire: "But it's all spent now."

Uncle: "You boys of today want too much money. Do you know what I was getting when I married your aunt?"

Nephew: "No, and I'll bet you didn't either."

He (making the time-worn excuse): "I'm afraid we'll have to stop here; the engine's getting pretty warm."

She: "You men are such hypocrites; you always say the engine."

Taxes

Everyone has wondered who hit Joe Louis hardest during his ring career. When asked, Joe simply shrugged his shoulders. "That's easy, Uncle Sam!"

When an old South African native was told he had to be taxed because the government, like a father, protected him from enemies, cared for him when he was sick, fed him when he was hungry, gave him an education, and for these purposes needed money, the old native said:

"Yes, I understand. It is like this: I have a dog and the dog is hungry. He comes to me and begs food.

"I say to him: 'My dear faithful dog, I see you are very hungry. I am sorry for you. I shall give you meat.'

"I then take a knife, cut off the dog's tail, give it to him, and say 'Here, my faithful dog, be nourished by this nice piece of meat.' "

One thing in favor of death over taxes—death doesn't get worse every time Congress meets.

Section 2

DEFINITIONS

Accountant: a party hired by a successful person to explain to the government how he did it.

Acrimony: what a man gives his divorced wife.

Advice: the approval sought for doing something one has decided to do.

Alarm clock: a small device used to wake up people who have no children.

Baby: an angel whose wings decrease as his legs increase.

Bachelor party: where a prospective bridegroom has the kind of wonderful time he could have every night if he weren't getting married.

Bank: 1. a place where you keep the government's money until the tax man asks for it. 2. an institution that urges you to save part of what you earn, and lends you money so that you can spend more than you earn.

Boss' son: the young man who is willing to start at the bottom for a few days.

Careful driver: 1. one who has just seen the man ahead get a traffic summons. 2. one who looks in both directions when he runs a red light. 3. a motorist on the way to court to pay a speeding ticket.

Cash: the poor man's credit card.

Child psychology: what parents use in letting their boys and girls have their own way.

College bred: something that's made from the flower of youth and the dough of old age.

Duty: a word used to excuse our delight in hurting others.

Economics expert: a man who knows tomorrow why the things he said yesterday didn't happen today.

Efficiency: using instant coffee to dawdle away an hour.

Exclusive club: a place where you can meet the kind of people you would have black-balled, if you'd have gotten in first.

Expert: one who has a good reason for guessing wrong.

Fanatic: 1. one who will stick to his guns whether they're loaded or not. 2. a fellow with such a large chip on his shoulder that it makes him lose his balance.

Father's Day: just like Mother's Day only you don't spend so much.

Free verse: the triumph of mind over meter.

Good executive: one who never does anything that he can get anybody else to do for him.

Grandparents: people who come to your house, spoil your children, and and then go home.

History: what enables each nation to use the other fellow's past record as an alibi.

Hotel: where you stay when you ain't got no cousins.

Ignoramus: a guy who doesn't know the meaning of a word you first learned yesterday.

Indispensable man: the motorist who whizzes past you just as you spot a motorcycle cop in the rear view mirror.

Intelligent conversationalist: one who nods his head in agreement while you're talking.

Juvenile delinquency: the result of parents trying to train children without starting at the bottom.

Leisure: the time you spend on jobs you don't get paid for.

Library: a place where the dead live.

Luck: good planning, carefully executed.

Luxury: something you do without until getting it, but by that time it has become a necessity.

Maternity dress: a space suit.

Maxim: a short rule of conduct made up by the rich to encourage the poor to keep on working.

Memory expert: a woman who has once been told another woman's right age.

Modern home: one that has half as much room for twice as much money.

Neighbor: a person who is always doing something you can't afford.

Nervousness: when you feel in a hurry all over and can't get started.

Obstacles: those frightful things you see when you take your eyes off the goal.

Old college classmate: someone who's gotten so bald and fat that he sees you at a class reunion and doesn't recognize you.

Opportunism: the ability to park on the other fellow's nickel.

Perfect guest: one who makes his host feel at home.

Perfect husband: one who is convinced he has a perfect wife.

Political bedfellows: men who usually use the same bunk.

Political promises: those that go in one year and out the other.

Praise: something a person tells you about yourself that you've suspected all along.

Prejudice: 1. being positive about something negative. 2. an unwillingness to be confused with the facts.

Propaganda: an opinion with which you do not agree.

Rabbit: a small animal that's here today and mink tomorrow.

Racehorse: the only animal that can take several thousand people for a ride at the same time.

Procrastinator: 1. one who puts off until tomorrow things he's already put off until today. 2. a person who can't put away the garden tools until the snow thaws.

Reckless driver: one who passes you on the highway, in spite of all you can do.

Research notes: things you keep for thirty years, then throw away the day before you need them.

Robber: what a doctor and a TV service man call one another.

Sadist: one who does kind things for a masochist.

School teacher: one who takes a lot of live wires and sees to it that they are well grounded.

Secretary: 1. a girl who can tell by a caller's name whether or not the boss is in. 2. a girl you pay to learn to type while she's looking for a husband.

Senior partner: the fellow who has nothing to do between trips to Florida; Junior partner: the boss' son.

Sentimentality: the name we give to any sentiment we are incapable of feeling.

Slogan: a good old American substitute for facts.

Snappy comeback: something you think of twelve hours after you were tongue-tied by somebody else's wisecrack.

So-and-so: the fellow driving the other car.

Social security: when a boy has the only football or baseball in the neighborhood.

Society folks: the upper crust, made from crumbs and held together by dough.

Spendthrift: a neighbor who makes more money than you do.

Section 3

TOASTS

Bride and Groom

To the Bride and Groom: May their troubles be little ones.

Here's to marriage—the gate through which the happy lover leaves his enchanted ground and returns from paradise to earth.

Companionship

Here's to the Have-beens, the Are-nows, and the May-bes!

Here's to my mother-in-law's daughter,
And here's to her father-in-law's son;
And here's to the vows we've just taken,
And the life we have just begun!

Here's to the bride that is to be,
Happy and smiling and fair,
And here's to those who would like to be,
And are wondering when and where.

Doctors

Here's to Medicine: The only profession that labors incessantly to destroy the reason for its own existence!

Fond of doctors, little health,
Fond of lawyers, little wealth.

The doctors are our friends, let's please them well,
For though they kill but slow they are certain.

Drinks—Eating

Let us have wine and women, mirth and laughter—
Sermons and soda-water the day after.

—Lord Byron

I drink to one, and only one—
And may that one be he
Who loves but one, and only one–
And may that one be me!

Fellowship

Here's to Hell! May we have as good a time there
as we had getting there.

Law—Lawyers

The Law: It has honored us; may we honor it!

—Daniel Webster

Here's to Justice—may she ever be swayed by the hand of mercy.

Here's to the Law—may it ever be a synonym for Justice.

—Justice Orrin N. Carter

Marriage

Here's to matrimony—the high seas for which no compass has yet been invented.

—H. Heine

Here's Health, Happiness and Harmony to every state in the *Union*—especially the married state.

'Tis better to have loved and lost
Than to marry and be bossed.

Mother-in-law

Here's to our dear old mother-in-law,
With all her freaks and capers,
For were it not for dear old ma,
What would become of the comic papers?

Old age

Only the good die young—Here's hoping that you live to a ripe old age.

Here's that we may live to eat the hen
That scratches on our grave.

Politics

Here's to the honest Politician—the man who when bought stays bought.

Press, The

Here's to the Press, the Pulpit, and the Petticoat, the three ruling powers of the day. The first spreads the knowledge; the second spreads morals; and the third spreads considerably.

Romance

Here's to this water,
  Wishing it were wine,
Here's to you my darling,
  Wishing you were mine.

Wife—Wives

To our sweethearts and wives. May they never meet!

Here's to our better halves,
Who reconcile us to our poorer quarters!

Here's to our wives, who fill our lives
  With little bees and honey!

They break life's shocks, they mend our socks,
  But don't they spend the money!

Woman—Women

Here's to Woman—she needs no eulogy; she speaks for herself.

Here's to Woman—the only sex which attaches more importance to what's on its head than to what's in it.

Here's to the first woman—who, if the legend be true, was only a side issue.

Here's to Woman—who came after Man, and who has been after him ever since.

Here's to woman—indestructible, delectable and—so deductible!

Here's to Woman—who generally speaking is generally speaking.

Here's to woman—ah, that we could fall into her arms without falling into her hands.

—AMBROSE BIERCE